The Art of Pleasure
A Sexual Technique

H.D. Hughes

Copyright © 2015 H.D. Hughes

All rights reserved.

ISBN: 069-252-0953
ISBN-13: 978-069-252-0956

DEDICATION

This writing is dedicated to my best friend, my best love, and my best friend for life. Thank you, you opened my eyes to the void we created in our lives. We were not sorry for our passion but for what we could not give each other. We will always love.

P—PEOPLE
L—LACKING
E—EFFECTIVE
A—AGGRESSIVE
S—SEXUAL
U—UNDERSTANDING
R—REPEATING
E—EXPERIENCED FAILURE

CONTENTS

	Acknowledgments	i
1	Pleasing	1
2	Kissing for Pleasure	3
3	Session one, towel one. Hot	8
4	Session two, towel two. Hot	9
5	Session three, towel three. Cold	8
6	Session four, towel four. Hot	11
7	Conclusion	12

ACKNOWLEDGMENTS

Markenna Seals: Editing
Carol Gray: Editing.
Linda Hughes: Editing

The Art Of Pleasure

I was told this about seven months ago. I have to admit at first I had my doubts. I thought sex could not get any better until I tried this technique. I explained it to my lady friend and she had doubts also. We then agreed to try it and both of us were pleasantly surprised. She was so overcome with pleasure that she actually cried. Now she asked for it whenever we have a sexual encounter.

R.L.H., Ashtabula, Ohio

This is my uncle, he told me about it sometime last year, I scoffed at the idea. Me I am young I don't need that to satisfy my girl. On a whim, I tried it the first time I got it wrong and had to call to get the steps right. During the first session I got it right I never got to the cold towel and man oh man what difference did it make. Tyr it with your girl I did with mine.

R.F., McComb, MS

I am a 51 year old woman who believed I knew my body and sexual pleasure was something that I could only achieve during long sessions of sexual activity. Well, one afternoon my girlfriend and I were shopping and I noticed something different about her. I commented that she looked different that's when she got this mischievous smile, so I asked if she was having an affair. She said no but her male friend had talked her into trying something called the "hot towel treatment". She went on to tell me how it increased her desire for passion and pleasure. Well, I had lots of questions which she explained and then told me how to do it. Well she was pleased and it really peeked my interest. I told my male friend about it. We tried it on a weekend getaway about a week or two later. OMG! It was so different and pleasing that I cried from the pleasure. I love this treatment, you must try it.

Linda, Woodbridge VA

I introduced my wife to the hot towel treatment last winter as something to spice up our sex life. She was curious, so I explained how the treatment works but did not explain the expected results. I told her how I learned of it and that, it was primarily for her pleasure and sexual enjoyment. She agreed to try it, she went wild and had a total of 3 intense orgasms. That was how she described the sensation and surge that went deeply through her body. We have made it a regular part of our sexual fore during and after play. Thanks to utilizing the hot towel treatment our sex life has been taken on a life of its own. "I would just like to say this treatment works. Try it yourself.

     M.K., Largo MD

"Simply Amazing" I call it the "Tune-Up" your girl will perform like never before. When I was told about this I laughed, thinking what can a hot towel do that I can't? Well out of curiosity, I tried it and to my surprise the results were outstanding. i could not believe my girl was there crying because of an orgasm she had. Our sex is much better. The hot towel treatment really works. Try it.

La Plata

    E.W. La Plata, Maryland

"I'm a 33 year old male and I considered myself experienced as far as the bedroom is concerned. I have dated my girl for 3 years and we had experimented with different sexual positions and toys. One day at the Tinder Box Cigar Bar, I was taking with some older gentlemen and as with most conversations in these settings, women and pleasure became the focus of our conversations. Each one had their way or ideas on pleasing a woman, one gentleman who was rather mute during the conversation asked if anyone of us had ever tried the hot towel treatment. He went on to explain how it worked and what we needed to do to achieve the desired results. He warned that it would drive a woman wild! About a week later, I explained to my girl and we tried it during foreplay. I was amazed and turned me on to see my lady squirm and moan. Needless to say she woke up the next morning and said that was the best night we ever had PERIOD. After breakfast she said she wanted to do it again.

    R. T., Washington DC

The Art Of Pleasure

I will tell you up front, I am a gay female. I thought I was totally in tuned with the wants and needs of my sexual partner and as a matter of fact with every female not that I am promiscuous, but because I am female dealing with females. I was of the opinion that satisfaction was second nature to me and nothing out there could out do me. Well, in my career field I am privileged to male conversation and that sometimes centers on sex and satisfaction. This one conversation I was privileged to, involved something called the hot towel treatment and how it elevates their female to new sexual heights, blab blab blab. I inquired about this treatment and because of my sexual orientation they were reluctant to share this information but eventually did. With me being in a female to female relationship, I am thinking yea, right. About two to three weeks later I talked my partner into trying it. Boy, did we get a surprise, our sexual appetite, our passion and ability to please each other increased and now we are regular participants in this fore, during and after play it is just that wonderful. Not only did I do it to her but she did it to me also and I experienced the most blissful climax I have had in a very long time. All I can say really is my, my, my. This is not child's play it is the real thing. Try it for yourself, I did.

F.T,. La Plata, MD

Pleasing

If you know how to please a woman sexually, you do not need this writing, maybe you should write your own. I am not speaking of sex alone. What I am speaking of is the actual pleasure we all seek. Understand this, pleasure is an art not a principle as some would suggest. it must be honed and sharpened repeatedly. Merriam-Webster defines pleasure as: a feeling of happiness, enjoyment, or satisfaction: a pleasant or pleasing feeling: activity that is done for enjoyment: something or someone that causes a feeling of happiness, enjoyment, or satisfaction. I define pleasure as the art of moving one to tears through sexual satisfaction.

I started this writing 45 years ago with my first sexual experience. Like most young boys, I had an older woman experience and sex was great but that's all it was just sex and a passion to cum, no pleasure. With that I went in search of the greatest sexual pleasure possible. over the years I had sex with different women of different races, creeds and colors and each left me a small piece of the puzzle I was constructing. Finally, it dawned on me that pleasure is not a principle but an art and women found pleasure in different things. Sucking their breast, licking vagina, anus, toes and other things in-between. I came to the conclusion that all these things were just a small part of the sexual act and had nothing to do with pleasure but more with sexual satisfaction. This is where I found my solution. I understood that sexual pleasure required different levels of intimacy for different women and the point that connected them and brought full pleasure was the art. The art described in this writing, I found worked no matter who the woman or man was depending on your sexual preference.

There is one exception and that is if your partner has opted out of the sexual experience or one that is so harden to the sexual experience these instructions will not work.

Before moving on, please be very selective upon whom you are applying these sexual practices. They work to perfection and can cause a bond to form and a relationship to strengthen. Enjoy.

KISSING FOR PLEASURE

A kiss is an expression of a pleasure. If you're like me you can never get enough of kissing, pecks, smooches, sensual or long and sexual. Kisses are the foundation of any great act and we know sex is an act that requires great skill if you want it to be a pleasure for you and your partner. In order to master the art of pleasure in the act of kissing we must first learn to appreciate the whole body and how to make it respond to the places we kiss. We skip the breast, the neck, the lips and the ears, these are areas that receive more attention than needed. As men we are not aware of what is called the hot zones (areas that bring instant pleasure and remembrance) and we miss the mark. In the art of pleasure these are essential to complete the pleasure package (the gift of pleasure). All of the following are not just hot spots but pleasure zones. Pleasure zones are zones that you never forget, they awakens the body to previous pleasurable acts. Kissable hot spots for a woman include the back of her hair line to the bottom her feet, her eyelids, the back of her ears and her fingers. The shoulders blades both sides, the spine, these should be kissed with tenderness and licked with an urgency while keeping in mind pleasure is never an urgent nor a hurried action but a desired effect. The sides of the body from the arms down to the sides of the ankle. One of the most underappreciated parts of a woman's body is the underside of the breast. This area is the third most sensitive part of her body. Give it lots of attention kiss it, lick it, suck it and nick it with your teeth, like a tender pinch. The side effect is a most desired response

Least we not forget, we must kiss her where she most desires it. We as men dive right in and again miss the pleasure zone in this area. I know, lets me explain. It begins with the lips of the vagina.

We must treat them just like the lips on her face. Kiss, suck, lick and nibble them she will appreciate the art. Do each one separately squeeze together suck, lick and nibble them. Remember this action is about the lips but not about the clitoris nor the inside of her vagina (that comes later with the hot towel treatment). We must also include the inside of the legs especially around the vaginal, I cannot emphasis enough the sensuousness of this area. We must remember the area between the anus and the vagina, the anus itself and last but not least the vagina. One technique I find that works well, is when you kiss the lips hold them together closing the clitoris in and kissing the lips like you would kiss the mouth without putting your tongue inside. Then individually kiss, lick, suck them, ride them up and down like you are playing a harmonica. Then lick the vagina watching her cum again and again if it is done correctly.

   Sex in and of itself is one means of pleasure and pleasure most assuredly is an art and it begins with understanding the body. Let's began with two knowns.
        1.   We know how to fuck.
2. Most people think they know how to make love.

   Leaving the latter up for debate. In making love one must get to a point where they know the body like its second nature.
Consider this, you are trying to make love to your partner it's always been intense but lately it's become mundane and you need to spice it up. Here is a simple solution that is sure to spark or rekindle your flame.

SESSION ONE TOWEL ONE

Imagine you and your girl are into it and you are giving her 100%. You have kissed her everywhere the breast, under the breast, the sides, the back up and down, both legs, the eye lids. She is now ready for intercourse. Well before you do, tell her to be patient and to stay in the same position. Get off the bed go to the bathroom get a face towel, run the water in the face bowl to the point where it's as hot as yours hand can stand maybe a little hotter but not too hot. Remember we are performing an art (pleasure). Wet the towel and ring it dry making sure to keep it tight in your hand. When you get back to the bed open her vagina lips place the hot towel between the lips, do not open the towel, making sure to place the tips of the towel on the clitoris and the vaginal opening. Keep it there for a few seconds as the towel cools, open the towel and use the remaining heat to gently wipe the insides of the vagina walls making sure to expose the soft interfolds of the vagina to the heat of the towel. Insert chapter four text here.

Session Two Towel Two

When the towel cools go back to the bathroom run the water hot again just as before go back to the bed this time unwring the towel and place it in the open lips of the vagina making sure the clitoris and the opening gets the heat by holding it in place. While the towel is still warm wipe in and around the anus while gently inserting a small part of the warm towel with the tip of your pointing finger in the anus. Before you get up for the third towel take a moment to lick and suck the clitoris gently. This is the point you began to you lick and suck the inside of the legs where vagina meets the legs on both sides. Once that is done no matter how hot she is or how much she wants you to fuck her at that moment don't do it proceed to the next step?

Session Three Towel Three

The next towel is what I call the shock towel. You may not get to this towel but if you don't, don't worry you've done a great job with the first two. Go back to the bathroom this time run the water cold, wring the towel as in the first step place the cold towel between the vagina lips with one tip on the clitoris and the other at the entrance to the vagina by holding it there. No matter how much she reaches for you do not let her touch you just yet. Unwring the cold towel and again wipe the vagina same as before. Before you go the bathroom for the last time slowly suck cold air and blow warm air over the clitoris like you are breathing through your mouth and the do the same with the vagina. Close the vagina lips and passionately suck or lick them. If all this is done correctly your lady will have cum at least three times but most assuredly once beyond belief.

Session Four Towel Four

Go back the bathroom this time run the water hot as you can stand again. Go back to bed keeping the towel rung place the towel tips one on the clitoris and the other at the entrance to the anus and press but not hard. Open the warm towel wipe the vagina making sure to insert a small part of the hot towel inside the vagina just like you were finger fucking and the anus. While you are doing this do not allow her to touch you sexually because this is about her pleasure not yours.

Conclusion

  Now the finishing touches began kissing her in all the orifices' mentioned before suck each vagina lip separately and then squeeze them and suck collectively. Kiss the inside of her legs where the vagina meets the thigh. Kiss the underside of her breast turn her over and suck or lick her back and the anus. Pointers try to avoid areas that make her laugh, this will cause you to believe this art is not working, but gentlemen is does.

  Finally gentlemen enjoy yourselves while you pleasure your partner for this pleasure is not returned. Ladies, relax take all pleasure. Let your man pleasure you and enjoy all the surprises this art will bring.

P—PEOPLE
L—LOVING
E—EFFECTIVE
A—AFFIRMATION
S—SEXUALLY (WHILE)
U—UPDATING
R—REPEATABLE
E—EXPERIENCES

The Art Of Pleasure

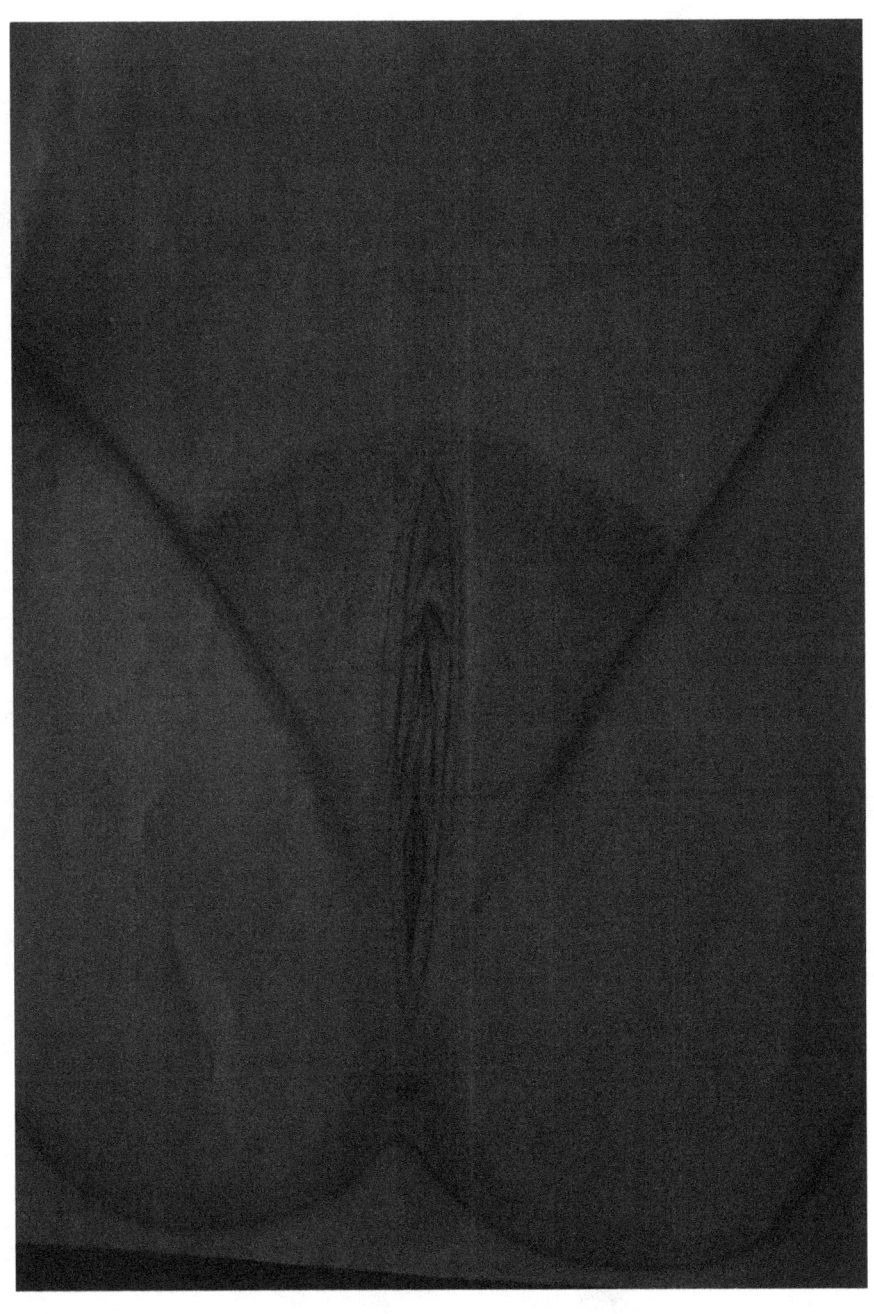

THIS IMAGE SHOWS WHERE TO PLACE THE HOT/COLD TOWEL IN MOST INSTANCES.
ILLUSTRATION 1

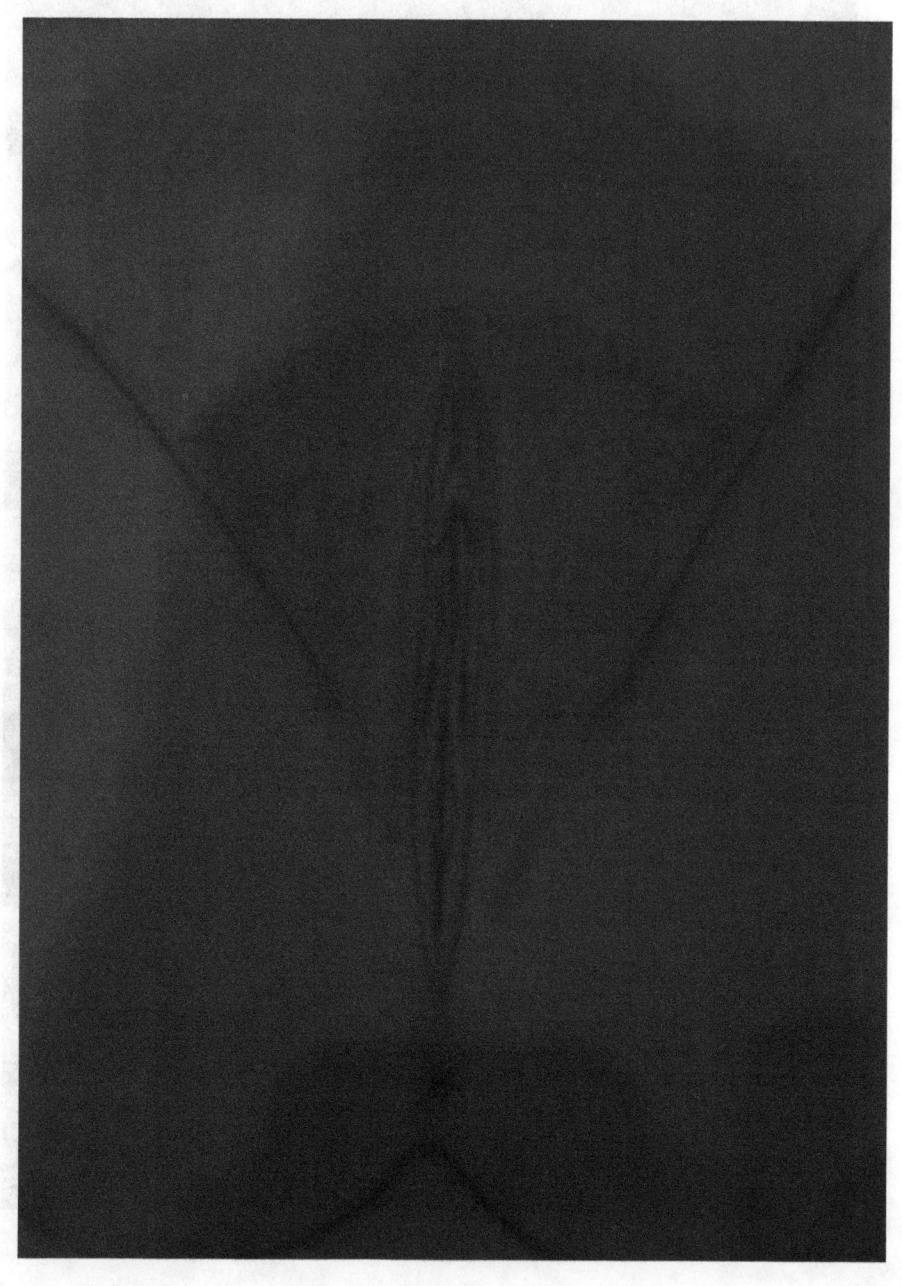

SUCK THE INSIDE OF HER LEGS WHERE THE VAGINA MEETS THE THIGH.
ILLUSTRATION 2

THE SIDES OF THE BODY FROM THE ARMS DOWN TO THE SIDES OF THE ANKLE.
ILLUSTRATION 3

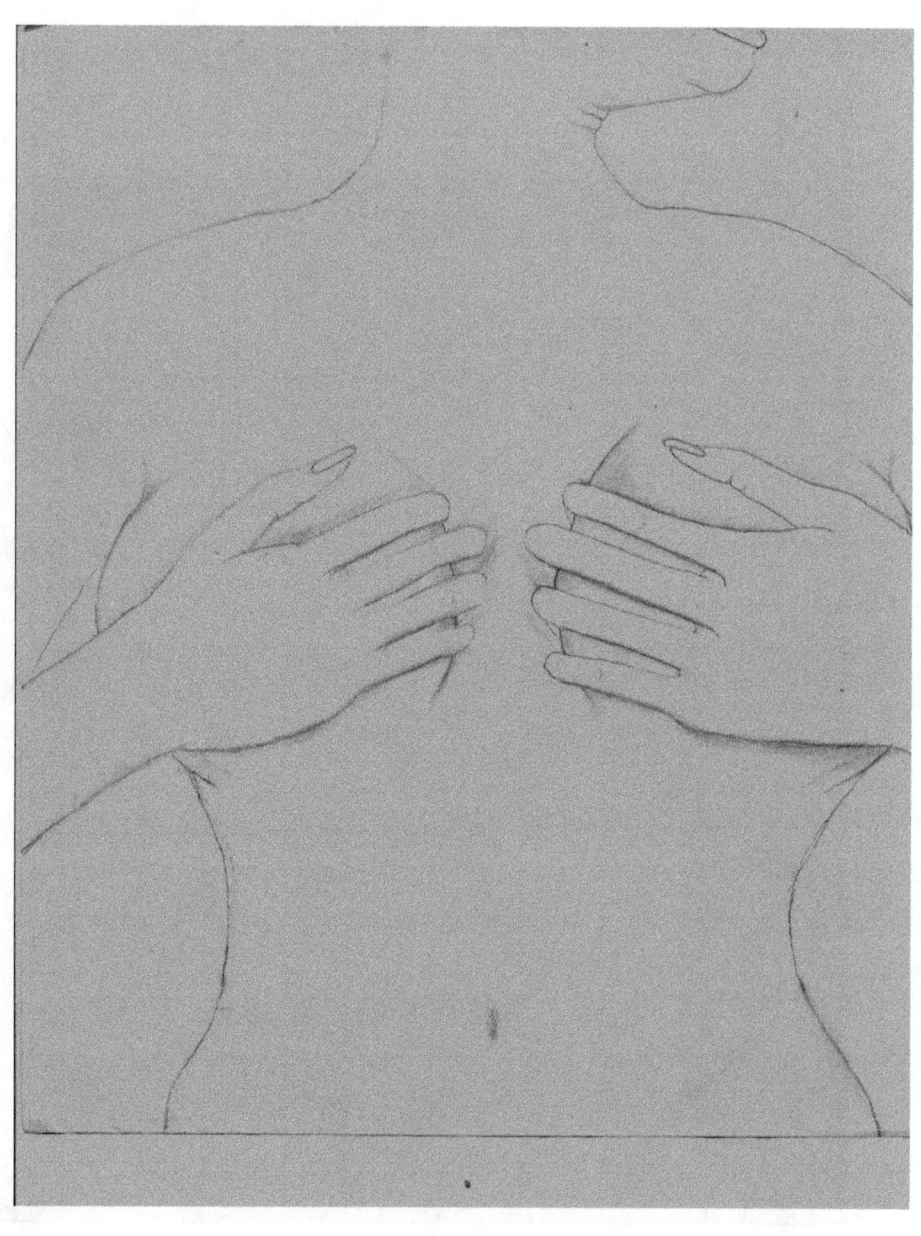

The underside of her breast. ILLUSTRATION 4

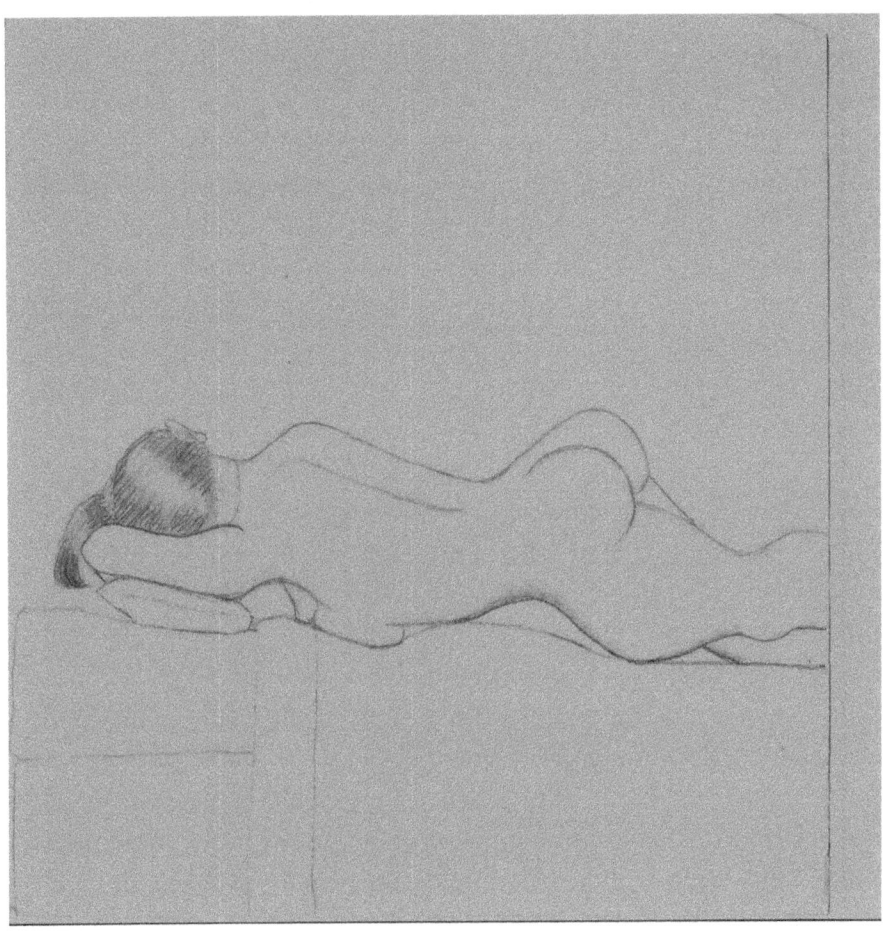

Suck or lick her back and her anus. Illustration 5

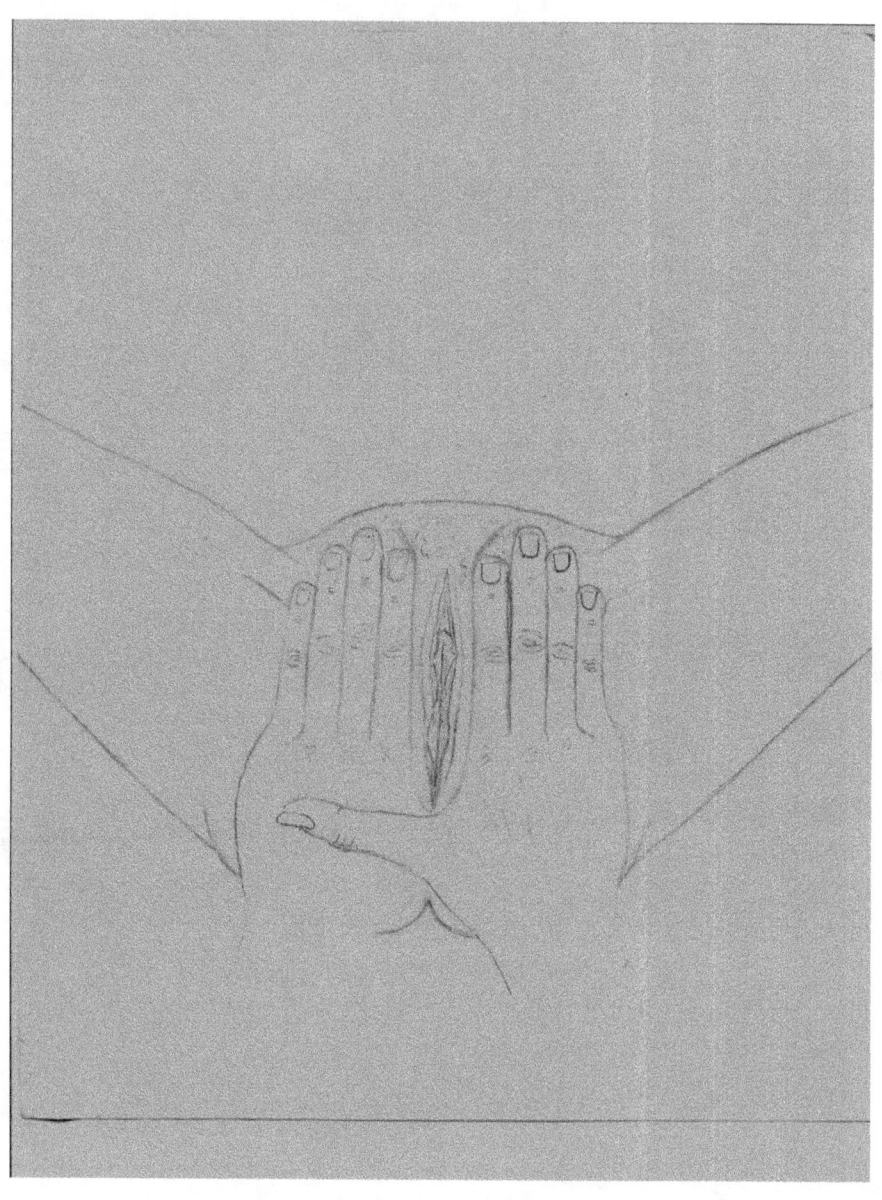

Kiss the lips hold them together closing the clitoris in and kissing the lips like you would kiss the mouth without putting your tongue inside.
Illustration 6

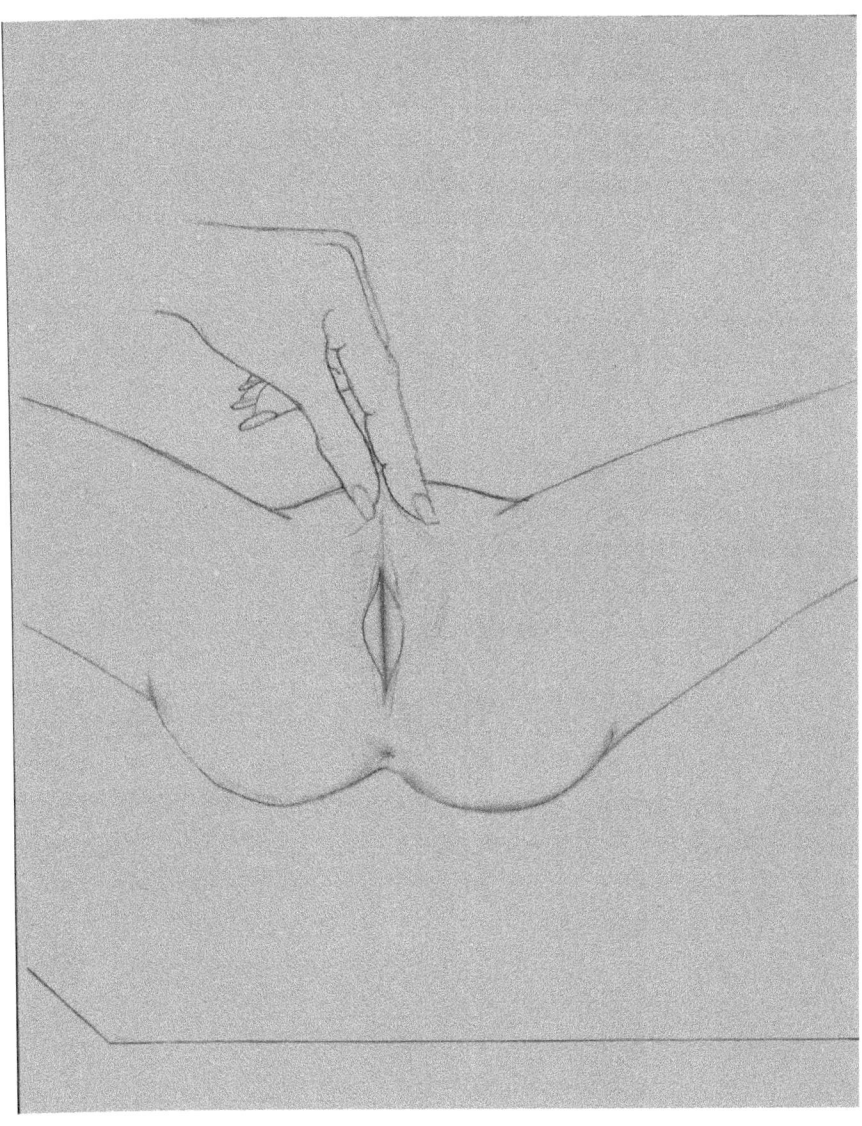

Kiss the lips hold them together closing the clitoris in and kissing the lips like you would kiss the mouth without putting your tongue inside.
Illustration 7

Herbert D. Hughes

Born July 1, 1955, in McComb, Mississippi. Now a resident of Washington DC

www.ingramcontent.com/pod-product-compliance
Lightning Source LLC
Chambersburg PA
CBHW071805040426
42446CB00012B/2716